Quarterback's
Adventure
in Alphabet Town

by *Janet McDonnell*
illustrated by *Jodie McCallum*

created by Wing Park Publishers

CHILDRENS PRESS ®

CHICAGO

Library of Congress Cataloging-in-Publication Data

McDonnell, Janet, 1962-
    Quarterback's adventure in Alphabet Town / by Janet
McDonnell ; illustrated by Jodie McCallum.
        p.   cm. — (Read around Alphabet Town)
    Summary: Quincy the quick quarterback saves the queen's
quacking duck from the quicksand and receives quites a reward.
Includes activities.
    ISBN 0-516-05417-1
    [1. Alphabet—Fiction.]   I. McCallum, Jodie, ill.   II. Title.   III.
Series.
PZ7.M1547Qu   1992
[E]—dc 20   92-1067
                                                  CIP
                                                  AC

Quarterback's
Adventure
in Alphabet Town

You are now entering Alphabet Town,
With houses from "A" to "Z."
I'm going on a "Q" adventure today,
So come along with me.

This is the "Q" house of Alphabet
Town. A quarterback lives here.
His name is Quincy.

Quincy loves "q" things. He has quite a few.

Quincy likes

quilts.

And he likes to collect

quarters.

But most of all, he likes to play
quarterback.

The fans are never quiet when
Quincy is on the field. They all
cheer for Quincy.

Quincy is the quickest quarterback around. He runs every day to stay quick.

One day when Quincy was running,
he heard a sound. "Quack, quack,
quack," went the sound.

Quincy looked to see where the quacks were coming from.

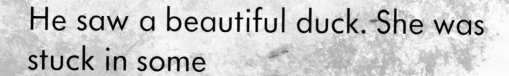

He saw a beautiful duck. She was stuck in some

quicksand!

"Quack! Quack!" cried the duck. She was sinking.

Quincy ran across the quicksand and grabbed the duck. He was so quick, he did not even sink.

Quincy was quite lucky that he
saved the duck. She was a magic
duck, so she could talk!

"Oh, thank you, thank you," said
the duck. "You saved my life."

"Where did you come from?" asked Quincy.

"I belong to a queen," said the duck.
"She lives at the top of a high hill.

"If you take me back to her, she
will give you a reward."

So Quincy took the magic duck back
to the queen.

The queen was very happy when she saw her magic duck. "Thank you, Quincy," said the queen.

"You are welcome," said Quincy.
"But I have a question. What else
can your magic duck do?"

"She lays magic eggs," said the
queen. "There is a quarter in each
one. And now I have a reward for
you."

The queen opened a big treasure
chest. It was filled with quarters!
"Wow!" said Quincy. "Thank you.

Now I have a gift for you too."
And he gave the queen two tickets
to the next football game.

When Saturday came, the fans
were quite surprised.

They had never seen a queen with a
duck at a football game before.

MORE FUN WITH QUINCY

What's in a Name?

In my "q" adventure, you read many "q" words. My name begins with "Q." Not many names begin with "Q." But here are a few.

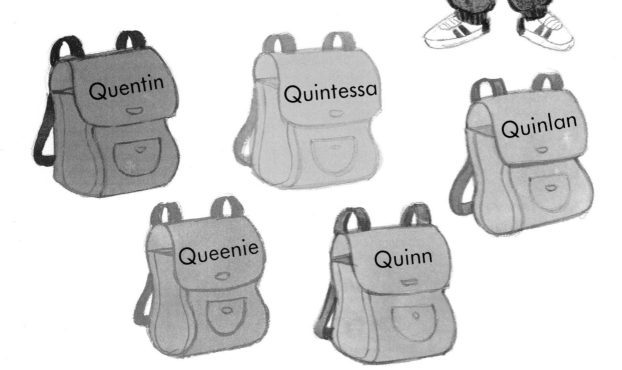

Do you know other names that start with "Q"?

Does your name start with "Q"?

Quincy's Word Hunt

I like to hunt for "q" words. Can you help me find the words on this page that begin with "q"? How many are there? Can you read the words?

gift

quail

goat

quart

question mark

quintuplets

What letter follows the "q" in each of the above words? That letter always follows "q." Can you find two words with no "q"?

Quincy's Favorite Things

"Q" is my favorite letter. I love "q" things. Can you guess why? You can find some of my favorite "q" things in my house on page 7. How many "q" things can you find there? Can you think of more "q" things?

Now you make up a "q" adventure.